Prince Edward Island

TRUE COLOURS

PHOTOGRAPHY BY
WAYNE BARRETT &
ANNE MACKAY

NIMBUS
PUBLISHING

Nimbus Publishing Limited
PO Box 9301, Station A
Halifax, NS B3K 5N5
(902) 455-4286

Design: Kate Westphal, Graphic Detail, Charlottetown, PEI
Printed and bound in Hong Kong by Everbest Printing Co. Ltd.

Nimbus Publishing acknowledges the support of the Canada Council and the Department of Canadian Heritage.

Canadian Cataloguing in Publication Data
Barrett, Wayne
Prince Edward Island
ISBN 1-55109-157-7
1. Prince Edward Island—Pictorial works. I. MacKay, Anne. II. Title.
FC2612.B37 1996   971.7'04'0222   C95-950316-1
F1047.8B37 1996

Acknowledgements:
We would like to thank the following for their assistance or information in the production of *True Colours:* Beverly Rayner, our trusted photographic assistant; Kate Westphal for her creative design contribution; Dorothy Blythe for the idea; Joanne Elliott for editing; Miles Boulter; Bryon Howard; Ebo Budu-Amoako, Food Technology Centre; Diagnostic Chemicals; PEI Department of Agriculture; PEI Tourism; PEI Museum and Heritage Foundation; Noel Potts; Leisa Way as "Anne of Green Gables"; Amy and Laura, our children, who graciously agree to pose continuously for us; and the numerous Islanders who have shared with us their favourite Island scenes.

Facing page: Potato fields stretch into the Northumberland Strait.

To my parents, Donald and Audrey MacKay, who continue to share with their grandchildren the same Island values and traditions that so influenced me.   —Anne MacKay

To my parents, Pearl and the late Allen Barrett, who so looked forward to their yearly visits to Prince Edward Island.   —Wayne Barrett

Wayne:

My first recollection of Prince Edward Island is vivid, enhanced by the kind of emotion only children possess. As a child, while curled up in a chair at my grandmother's, I opened the *Star Weekly* (a publication discontinued many years ago), and spread over the pages before me was a portrait of a landscape so tranquil and beautiful, it left a lasting impression on my young imagination. It was a photo essay of Prince Edward Island by the late Island artist Mark Gallant. I longed to then someday see this enchanted place for myself and maybe learn to capture its beauty on film.

At the age of twenty-one, and for the first time in my life, I left my childhood home of Cape Breton and began my career as a photographer in the Canadian Armed Forces. Destiny landed me here on this little Island that had so inspired me years earlier in my grandmother's parlour. It was on a bleak and blustery day in October that my seasoned sergeant informed me I would never leave this place and declared I would marry an Island girl. His prediction was like a wizard's spell upon me; I was defenceless. At the time, I scorned his words as I had big plans to travel the world and not settle down. Twenty-seven years later, I am delighted to admit his prophesy came to pass. I have lived here ever since, and I am married to an Islander. (My spouse informs me I should write, "happily married.") I find I am also defenceless when it comes to her.

I consider myself a Prince Edward Islander along with my wife, Anne, and our three children, Jason, Amy, and Laura, all of whom have lived and grown up on this Island. Although, there was a time, several years ago, when my son informed several guests that we were all Islanders in the family, "but Dad was not." I might expect this kind of statement from others, but it was a surprise from my own son! After some parental persuasion, something to do with him getting dessert, he agreed to change his statement.

Prince Edward Island has moulded my family, my career, and me in profound ways. The people, with their love of place and pride in their Island home, have taken me in and made me part of their family, a family whose relations spread so far and wide, it leaves me thinking I must now be related, in some distant way, to everyone here.

Inhabitants who have moved away and visitors to Prince Edward Island carry with them a nostalgia and emotional force that draw them back. This place has inspired many artists and writers. The most famous, of course, is Lucy Maud Montgomery, whose evocative descriptions of the people and landscape are read by millions all over the world. The power and charm of the place is seen in the eyes of a Japanese

girl waiting backstage at Confederation Centre as she meets the actress who plays the enviable roll of Anne of Green Gables, and on the sun-warmed faces of visitors enthralled as they watch the setting sun wash red the sandstone cliffs on the north shore. I am thankful to live in such a place. I thank Mark Gallant for my first impressions of this Island and the sergeant who saw a future for me that I had no idea would be mine.

Anne:

From my earliest memories, I was indoctrinated to become an Islander who would spend her life in this place. My father would tell me bedtime stories of the olden days in Pleasant Valley, the Depression years, family history, farming adventures, and of course, Old Tony, his prize workhorse. And at the age of twelve, my childhood dream came true when I received a pony for Christmas, a pony I put in the same class as great steeds like Black Beauty.

Looking back now, I recall a potbellied, scruffy, stubborn, little Shetland pony, which I would have named Tony, if she hadn't already been named. She transformed my life and took me on many adventures in the back fields and woods where I spent most of my adolescent years riding. I lived each day to be in the woods and along tractor paths behind neighbouring farms. I would sit for what seemed like hours on

horseback, overlooking wonderful scenes. (These moments were often the result of a stubborn pony, unwilling to move, but they gave me time to appreciate the view.)

The first transforming memory I have of the Island landscape is during a ride on a dreary spring evening. Upon galloping to the crest of a hill, the black clouds pulled back from the horizon, the sky flooded with gold, and the red fields became surreal. The wind ceased; I was suspended in a timeless moment.

Countless times since then, I have witnessed similar scenes here on the Island and have spent many years trying to capture on film those moments and the accompanying moods.

Perhaps the most beautiful time of day is the hour leading up to and including sunrise. For those of us fortunate enough to live in a rural setting, the experience is unrivalled.

A vibrant patchwork of colours is revealed as the fog disappears over the Southwest River.

Facing page: A carpet of gold and green leads to the sea at Park Corner.

To step down off the verandah into the engulfing silence and to look up into a blue-black sky filled with twinkling stars is an experience that inspires reverence. The few who dare to venture out at such an hour are rewarded with calm and peace. For the photographer, this kind of peace is carried within and is portrayed in the photos taken at this tranquil time of day. In the moments just before the leading edge of the sun touches the horizon, light floods through the hollows and hills and creates a magical setting.

During the first cold night of autumn, the ground fog stirs and develops into a golden swirling mist that is suspended in the sunrise hours. The lay of the land, with its gentle hollows and rolling hills dotted with farms, hedgegrows, and winding rivers present the photographer with a scene that nearly defies capture by a camera. In these moments, I often wonder if what I am experiencing can

possibly be conveyed on film. It is with sheer discipline that I pull my eyes away from such a scene and attempt to photograph it.

Every part of the Island is beautiful: the windswept cliffs of North Cape, the colourful Acadian festivals, the gentle rolling potato fields dipping down to the sea near DeSable, the historic site of Province House where our country had its beginnings, the north shore with its unending dunes, the world-class golf course at Crowbush Cove, and the East Point Light that shines over the Gulf of St. Lawrence.

Prince Edward Island is our home and we are proud to live here.

Anne MacKay and Wayne Barrett

P.S. Yes, we really are married to each other.

Lupins, in vivid shades of purple, pink, and white, line a Margate roadside.

Facing page: Dawn turns a pond to gold in Marshfield.

Rhythmic movement of the waves sculpts the south shore's red sand.

Facing page: Majestic cliffs rise out of the sea in Norway.

A church steeple in Hunter River, cloaked in fog, waits for the sun to brighten its view.

Facing page: A lonesome gull awaits his fisherman friend.

Lobster boats rest while recreationers venture out into New London Bay.

Facing page: A lighthouse shines brightly in Covehead.

Providing spectacular vistas in virtually every direction, Park Corner is the site of Lucy Maud Montgomery's fictional "Lake of Shining Waters."

Facing page: John Barrett's brilliant sunflowers adorn the landscape of New Dominion.

Island artists create a bounty of beautiful crafts such as this pottery created by Peter Jansons, owner of the Dunes Studio Gallery in Brackley Beach, and his assistant Joel Mills.

Facing page: The Southwest River winds gracefully in the distance and in the foreground colourful lupins line a roadside in Clinton.

A crimson maple leaf floats lazily on a pond's surface.

Facing page: You can still come upon lovely old clay roads climbing age-old hills, and woodlands much like this scene near Crapeau.

Only the moon dares to brave the cold on a frosty winter's day in Norway.

Facing page: For a fleeting moment, both sun and moon grace opposite horizons in Meadowbank.

Morning dew shimmers on a fern found on the Balsom Hallow Trail behind Green Gables house in Cavendish.

Facing page: A mass of brilliant lupins competes to be the tallest against a blue summer sky.

*Island fiddler Miles Boulter plays
a jig at Canoe Cove.*

*Facing page: By noon, the boats
have all returned to port in Naufrage.*

This well-known old light in Cape Tryon commands one of the Island's most spectacular views overlooking the Gulf of St. Lawrence.

Facing page: Kayaker Bryon Howard of Outside Expeditions discovers the sea-formed caves along the coastline of Kildare.

A Meadowbank farm is immersed in the blue cast of a full moon.

Facing page: Each season after the first snowfall, Queenie and Sandy are hitched to the sleigh to chauffeur guests through the snow-covered woods on Pott's Farm in Bonshaw.

An Island feast of fresh lobster.

Facing page: A sunny veranda marks the entrance to the PEI Preserve Company in the picturesque village of New Glasgow.

A country lane in Dunstafenage, with leaves blown into grass-lined crevices, is colourfully inviting.

Facing page: The evening light produces a brilliant reflection at Stanley Bridge.

Researcher Ebo Budu-Amoako studies samples at the Island's Food Technology Centre.

Facing page: A chemist at Diagnostic Chemicals checks her work.

Best friends frolic in the waves at Newfrage.

Facing page: Cavendish Beach— a perfect playground.

Canola ripens on a sunny afternoon in lot 16.

Facing page: Different stages of growth and harvesting create flowing ribbons of crops in Chepstow.

After a summer storm, the air is filtered with a special quality of light, bathing Cumberland in a warm and inviting glow.

Facing page: Autumn mist hangs in the hollows on a balmy fall morning in Clyde River.

Cyclers abandon their travels to test the refreshing waters off East Point.

Facing page: A panoramic view of land and sea from the TransCanada Highway in DeSable.

The Blockhouse Light is located at the mouth of Charlottetown Harbour. Built in 1877, it is now a private home.

Facing page: Final moments of an evening sunset silhouette the diminishing sandbars of Canoe Cove as the tide retreats.

The last vibrant lights of dusk disappear behind an Island farm in Brookfield.

Facing page: Winter snow shows evidence of a red fox having passed along the shore of the National Park in North Rustico.

The Links at Crowbush Cove is one of the most beautiful golf courses in North America. This undulated landscape is snuggled in the dune-lined shore of St. Peter's Bay.

Facing page: The view from the 11th hole is both breathtaking and commanding.

A collection of shells at Rice Point.

Facing page: A golden sunset washes over Cavendish Beach— the perfect end to a perfect day.

On a slope of pasture in Hunter
River, two Ayreshire cattle keep one
another company.

Facing page: Grand River—
a tranquil setting for St. Patrick's
Parish, one of the Island's many
landmark churches.

Apple blossoms fill the branches of a tree along this street in Wellington.

Facing page: Red, white, and blue banners mark the entrance of Prince Edward Island's Acadian Museum in Miscouche.

Spinnaker's Landing on the Summerside Harbour is an active backdrop for an afternoon stroll.

Facing page: An aerial view of Summerside Harbour.

A sly red fox in St. Catherines. Better lock the barn tonight.

Facing page: A lone tree in the fading February sun.

The Confederation slips through a narrow passage as it leaves Wood Islands for Caribou, Nova Scotia.

Facing page: A bird's eye view of Cousins Shore.

Leisa Way as Anne of Green Gables.
Lisa portrayed the character of
Anne in the Charlottetown Festival
for several years.

Facing page: Millions of people have
visited Green Gables since it became
one of Canada's National Parks.

A sign on a fishing boat in North Rustico Harbour demonstrates the unique Maritime sense of humour.

Facing page: A New London lighthouse in the soft glow of morning.

The delicate sand dunes of Cable Head are now protected under the stewardship of the Island Nature Trust.

Facing page: A willet pauses in the ocean waves.

The quiet waters of the New Glasgow River mirror the autumn evening's tranquility.

Facing page: These red fields in Long River will soon be green with the arrival of spring.

Breathtaking fall foliage reflects in a pond in Mill River.

Facing page: Vibrant colours radiate from this row of back yard maple trees in Cornwall.

The Island has many lovely Bed
& Breakfast locations, including
the Elmwood Heritage Inn in
Charlottetown.

Facing page: A gentle morning dove
takes shelter in a sleeping lilac bush
in St. Catherines.

The interior of Beaconsfield, the home of the Island's Museum and Heritage Foundation, celebrates Christmas—Victorian-style.

Facing page: Charlottetown's historic Province House illuminated for the festive season.

Strip-farming practices create contrast and design to this lush landscape along the ocean's edge.

Facing page: Farmers work together in Victoria to harrow the Island's deep rich soil.

Garden plants covered in glistening winter frost.

Facing page: The Island's provincial bird, the Blue Jay.

Potato fields and sky converge on a distant farm in Chepstow.

Facing page: A farmer harvests grain in the fields overlooking French River.

A street musician entertains passers-by at Peake's Quay on Charlottetown's waterfront.

Facing page: A lighthouse stands at the mouth of New London Bay, where the sailing ship Marco Polo met its fate.

Overleaf: A country lane leads to a farm in Cumberland.